Chaotic Nightclub Photos: The Review

Gabrielle de la Puente

ROUGH TRADE BOOKS

We're in a nightclub. It's British, generic. Pretty white, working class, and very straight by the looks of things. This could be Newcastle or anywhere; Liverpool but not Rome. It's heaving. The songs are the songs from the radio, just sped up and played ten times louder. The drinks are cheap and everybody has one; gold and blue liquids poured into big plastic cups that will eventually be dropped onto the floor, splitting into sticky plastic shards underfoot and heel. What time is it? No one gives a shit. It's dark and then it's too bright, especially if you blink in time with the strobe lights. It's going to be a fucking nightmare to clean up. The toilets smell competitively of bleach, aftershave and piss; the girls form life-long, night-long bonds in the queue and then never see each other again.

The crowd is drunk, happy, horny and nervous, too. There's a girl at the centre of the action. She stands out with her crown of bright red hair. Her eyeshadow is a complementary orange that blooms over white skin, and we can see the make-up clearly because she has her eyes closed and everything in the world is still. Her face looks so at peace. There's a tall man pressed up behind her, breathing heavily into an ear, leaning down to kiss her neck. He might definitely have something to do with that expression, the way she makes the room look quiet—an expression we think we might want for ourselves, yeah. We think we might want to be her. He's feeling her chest with both hands so intensely that we can see veins taut on the back of them. She is stunned, ascending for all we know. The club is a gateway to Elysium. We wonder if we can come too.

They should probably get a room, these two. Actually, privacy might undo what's happening here. Another girl who could be a friend or a stranger is holding a vodka red bull in one hand and pointing directly at us with the other. Her pupils are completely dilated, but we won't tell. Inexplicably, there is an old man in a suit next to the three of them looking like he has walked into the wrong venue—or maybe it's exactly the right one; his cheeks are flushed, his eyebrows are raised, and his shirt is mostly undone. Excellent. They are the supporting cast. Behind, the background actors are mid-wave with their hands in the air, buoyed by radio-tested music. They have no idea what is happening right next to them because they're too busy opening gateways for themselves.

The red-headed girl is the main character in this scene. Her door is cracked open, light is shining through, and as the audience, we're witnessing foreplay for a Pre-Raphaelite, or the *Ecstasy of Saint Theresa*. Onlookers caught mid-action, everybody arranged dramatically in order to tell us an important story. Listen up! Stop what you are doing and glare! Except... this isn't a famous painting in a museum or a protected sculpture in a church in Italy. This isn't a still from a music video or a perfume advert, or some performance in a sweaty D.I.Y. art space. No, this is the perfect result of nightclub photography in modern Britain, and everyone is glowing because of the hot white flash of the DSLR camera.

On 20th March 2022, a Twitter account appeared called Chaotic Nightclub Photos, also known as @ClubPhotos_. In the opening of this text, I have described the very first image it posted—an image which helped it gain over 300,000 followers in its first week. Fifty tweets in, one million followers. No words, no captions. The account shares real images and videos every few days, or a few times a day if we're lucky. The mysterious account holder farms content from across the internet, recycling previously popular tweets, pulling images from subreddits, and also taking submissions in direct messages from followers who want to support the mission.

And listen, I know you've just opened this pamphlet ready to be a well-behaved, offline, healthy person who reads acoustic words IRL but I am giving you permission to take out your phone and find Chaotic Nightclub Photos on Twitter. Because yeah, I can try my best to describe the scenes, and I'll enjoy trying, but there is something rabid about the experience of seeing this content in full colour. It is like witnessing some intense PDA, or seeing someone have a shit in public; or when you're on the bus and the person next to you is listening to Adele on full blast, not realising the headphones they've got on aren't actually connected to their phone. It's about experiencing something you probably weren't supposed to take part in. Absurd, engaging, *chaotic*.

That's what it *feels* like, but if you don't have your phone to hand—or God forbid the account is taken down—this is what it *looks* like. Get ready.

A woman tries to deepthroat an entire beer bottle while a man looks on in horror. Another woman in a green dress tries to deepthroat her own hand. A man in a leather jacket swings his arms up in the air while a woman in chunky blue heels flies upside-down through the air over his head. A different man stands at a different bar. The staff serving him have no idea he is pissing on the floor in front of it. A girl smiles innocently for the camera but she has no idea there's a woman setting her hair on fire. Another hand disappears into another mouth. A white boy smiles, the tip of his nose and cheeks printed with the foundation of the Black girl smiling beside him (the placement of the colour makes him look like a smitten little clown). Similarly, a group stand in a line to pose for the camera. Two of the three men have a blur of pink lipstick around their mouths that matches that one girl's make-up in the centre. A man smiles as his front tooth falls out of his mouth, caught in mid-air by the flash. And you know those urinals that look like troughs that animals might eat out of, the ones that are metal and hard and cold? Well, there's a man fast asleep inside one of them. There's also a dog in the club.

Everyone looks like they are having the time of their lives, including the dog. And I scroll, and I scroll, and I scroll.

At face value, the reason I enjoy the account so much is because the images are funny. Some of them are a mystery, and occasionally they're even beautiful. Why is there a dog in the club? Did these people survive the night? What luck to catch the falling tooth on camera! And what actually happened when that guy woke up in his toilet bed? I want to know the answer in great detail. Because I don't imagine he would have to lie there very long for the yellow smell to absorb into his polo shirt and Primarni jeans. I wonder if he had trouble getting a taxi home because of the incident, if he had to walk the whole way back, if he ever got the smell out or if he just outright binned his clothes. I wonder if I should spend my time wondering these things, but here we are.

The account makes me think of the antics I once got up to in huge heels and tiny dresses when I was still learning to drink (and afterwards). I'd spend free periods on Fridays with a palette on my knee in the school common room colour-matching the pale green of my provisional driver's license so that I could change the 4 in 1994 to a 1. I'd do it to my card and then to everybody else's in sixth form; the acrylic paint would sometimes chip off in our purses and need resetting. But we were desperate to be let in. Desperate to fool the bored security guards so that we could blow off A-Level steam once inside. Chaotic Nightclub Photos has me wondering if any pictures starring my 17-year-old self are still online. 19 and at a full moon party in Thailand. 21 and single in university. I start to hope they are not, and then I remember I am 29 now, I've been ravaged by life, and no one could even recognise me.

And I imagine this reaction can be applied to many people who follow the account. *Ha ha, don't we look ridiculous when we drink?* It's relatable, entertaining content—that's its worth and that could be the end of this essay. But I'm still looking at the red-headed girl in the club. I'm still watching videos of men secretly standing on their tip-toes while they try to keep up with the majesty of heels. It's like this, right—occasionally I'll notice something particularly mad happening in culture and stop. Because I personally enjoy the thing, and happen to have the arbitrary power of a critic, I'll decide it's my responsibility to figure out what it is doing for the sake of posterity, the audience, and myself. That's what critics are good for, I think. Mapping it all out. In this case, I am convinced there is more to my intrigue than *relatability*, because there are a million other relatable accounts and none of them feel as pertinent.

For as long as there have been nightclubs, artists have been chronicling what goes on inside of them. This is very funny to me because I know artists, and most of them are serious people with bedtimes. To imagine them embedded on dance floors throughout history makes me feel somewhat relieved, and also vindicated when I encourage artists to get weirder.

Speaking of weirdness, as much as I'd like to see the image of a rat-arsed Victorian man deepthroating his friend's pocket watch for the banter, or the bants, or whatever the kids are saying nowadays—the image I crave, painted intricately in oils and framed ornately with gold, simply does not exist. People have always had a bevvy, that much is true. In the side-on art of Ancient Egyptians, the liquid is flowing 2D-style; and it's still flowing when we swing by the art-on-pots era of the Ancient Greeks. But in the long lineage of art history that precedes Chaotic Nightclub Photos, drunken art is generally, surprisingly, relatively calm. *Pour liquid in vessel. Raise vessel to thine mouth.* There are pre-nightclub artworks that do stir my soul a tad. Jacob Jordaens had a go in *The Feast of the Bean King* from 1640-1645. There's a figure in the foreground on the left doing a sneaky vom, but you might not even notice if I hadn't told you; plus, there's an inscription in the back of the room that reads *nil similus insano quam ebrius*, meaning nothing is more like a madman than a man who is drunk. The joke's on us for not speaking Latin. Matteo Ghidoni's *Interior of a Tavern with a Fight between Drunks* (painted some time between 1675-1689) also has a good sloppiness to it; and Francisco Goya has *The Drunken Mason* from 1786, in which two men grin while they carry their inebriated mate who has seemingly lost his pants. Good for him.

Yeah, drinking's been happening in art for as long as there has been drink to be had (Jesus, that sentence sounds drunk, which is why I'm going to leave it like that). But that tactical vomit, and the double-vision fist fight, and the mysterious loss of one's trousers—those details are few and far between. Is it because past generations were relatively calm even when they let their hair down? Or were the chaotic

An 8-second Snapchat video labelled 'my point of view as a DJ' shows a drunk girl rubbing her face up and down and left and right across the perspex shield in front of the DJ booth 💊 She looks like a pig, and then a ghost, and then a pig again, her nose and mouth stretching against the screen 🪩 She also looks like she is going to have rubber burns (and nightclub germs) right across her face when this is over 🍺 Taylor Swift sings 💃💃💃 *but I keep cruising, can't stop, won't stop movin'* over the speakers 🎵

nighttime activities of the past not allowed to make it into the cultural imaginary of the time because of societal norms and religious control? It's my go-to for every problem in life but I once again blame the bourgeoisie. Art back then (as right now) was often only able to exist if it was commissioned. Commissioners back then (as right now) aren't going to splash the cash to depict their mate after one too many meads. Commissioners want to garner respect and academic reverence through the artworks they have a hand in. They want ye olde clout! And to get it, they're going to need paintings that seem wealthy and serious. People being very well behaved. Gods, horses, really big fields. Nobody is having a laugh, and the canon feels worse off for it (as art always does when artists aren't just bankrolled to make whatever madness they really want to make).

Once nightclubs as we know them finally opened their doors, the art kept suffering from this hangover of dry propriety. It's kind of sad because it makes everyone in the past look like they had shit nights out, even if that wasn't the case. Original nightclub art is tame but I want to briefly describe some of it to you before we delve into the relevance of Chaotic Nightclub Photos. That's because I think it goes a long way towards explaining why the account has ended up hitting my present tense body so hard. There is a huge jump between classical art and the imagery on this Twitter account, and I think it's useful to feel the distance, because this shit isn't normal, and its newness is an important aspect to underline.

I'll put it this way. In July 2020, @cal_gif tweeted, 'what modern day thing do you think would kill a victorian era child? I think a single sip of 4loko would wipe them out.' Four Loko is an infamous American 12% alcoholic energy drink that sends college students off their heads. Cal's tweet launched one of my favourite memes of all time. It invites the internet to collectively think of the harsh, intense elements of modern day existence that we take for granted even in their potency—elements that some un-vaccinated child from the olden days just couldn't survive. If Cal's meme is an exercise in time-travel, I believe a glimpse of a Chaotic Nightclub Photos tweet could wipe one of those translucent kids right out.

The earliest nightclubs appeared in New York in the 1840s. An article in a 1927 issue of The New Yorker reflected on 'When New York Was Really Wicked' with engravings of concert saloons from the 1860s. These saloons 'provided dancing and liquor, but the principal attractions were the waiter girls and the low theatrical performances, although some of the cheaper establishments, particularly those along the Bowery, offered as entertainment only a piano virtuoso, who was always drunk and was always called the Professor.' Music, bevvies, and women serving the men; time is a flat circle. In the engravings—and in the writing—everyone is seated and fully clothed. You probably would have assumed that but given the subject, I had to make it clear. The other day, Chaotic Nightclub Photos shared a picture of a girl pulling her own skirt up to take a photo of her crotch. It currently has 81,000 likes. It is sobering to look back at a world in black and white. It is kind of boring too.

If we follow the timeline from those early New York clubs like the dutiful readers we are, we arrive in France post-La Belle Époque. Édouard Manet's last major work painted in 1882 shows a blonde barmaid front and centre at the Folies-Bergère. This was a bar offering entertainment ranging from ballet to circus acts, and where the barmaids were assumed to be sex workers on the down-low. The down-low stays there, sort of. There is a mirror behind the woman and we can see in the greyed out reflection that she is being approached by a man. He stands where we are, as if we are approaching her with the same request. Deeper into the reflection, we can see people sitting at tables under huge chandeliers, as well as the dangling feet of a trapeze artist. The chaos of the nightclub is still relatively restrained in its depiction, even when its subject is on the verge of saying much more.

Picking up where Manet left off, Henri de Toulouse-Lautrec was famously painting Parisian nightlife as early as 1888, showing us dancers kicking their legs at the Moulin Rouge around the corner from Manet's gaff. In his cabaret and café bar paintings, there are crowds pressed up against one another with abstract lines to indicate movement and flow around the room. When it came to other parts of Montmartre's night time economy, Toulouse-Lautrec was all-in, painting half-naked women with their customers. If you've still got your phone lying around and you've been checking out each of these works as we go, search for *Brothel on the Rue des Moulins Rolande*, 1894. A man is lost in the bedding between the legs of a woman. Ooh la la! Back downstairs, the artist was honouring the dancers, and the lighting, and the lateness of all this activity. And it's less *Ooh la la!* and more *okay, then*. That's some people in a club. Moving on.

In another part of the world in the exact same year, the Brooklyn Daily Eagle was describing another of New York's first nightclubs, Webster Hall, with lovely seediness. According to the reporter, Webster Hall was 'a big, bare, dingy place, where all the year round discontented men meet to discuss their wrongs and sympathise with one another, and where secret societies and political organisations, labour unions and similar associations make a business of pleasure. It is a grimy neighbourhood, where the rattle of retail trade continues all day and leaves poverty to toss itself to sleep at nightfall.' I read that and thought... *excellent, I hope someone was taking photos. I hope there is evidence that we have always been unhinged, and that artists have always been there to capture our mad recreation.* But the earliest images of Webster Hall by photographer Jessie Tarbox Beals, likely taken in the early 1900s, just show girls lined up in a costume ball, lightly holding each other's dresses in a procession. Technology is partly to blame, because subjects would have had to stand nice and still for the camera for a deadeningly long time. I guess this also excuses the painters to some extent...

In John Sloan's 1907 painting of people walking into the Haymarket club in New York, there is a sign above the door illuminating the entrance, and the hint of dancing through the windows, but the artist stays put outside. It's a cosy depiction. *Cosy*. Nowhere near a man's body being chilled by the sharp metal box of a urinal. (I really need to know what happened). Over in Europe, Zürich's artsy nightclub Cabaret Voltaire was coming to life and then closing its doors all in the year 1916. I say artsy because the space is dubbed the birthplace of Dadaism. There were exhibitions and performances, and the small amount of imagery that exists makes it look more gallery than nightclub. Different kind of experimentation going on in there.

Over in Berlin, Jeanne Mammen was painting carnival crowds in the 1920s with a covert focus on lesbian couples dancing closely, head to head, all dressed up and bright. Why does it all seem so cute? Like, God bless the cotton socks of people who lived in a world before raves. Where are the bodily fluids? Why do I miss them? On my internet travels from the 20s onwards, I only found steadfast photojournalism and archival footage of nightlife that dealt in keeping up appearances.

Even when I arrived at the late 70s Studio 54 era of glamorous celebrity-exclusivity, and even though there are stories of sex on the club's balcony, open drug use, and child actors getting pissed before their time, the pictures stay so incredibly clean. Grace Jones is wrapped in a huge piece of glittering blue fabric that comes down from a headdress to twist around her waist; Dolly Parton strokes a white horse in the club, except it seems kind of casual that there's a horse in the club; and then Bianca Jagger arrives on another horse to celebrate her 30th birthday. I guess this establishment was used to their horses? Because with the style of the images and the guests starring in them, everything looks editorial, staged, romantic, and sort of unreal. That is to say, none of it is chaotic, just rich, and richly dreamlike.

There are some topless women making their way through the club during a special Folies Bergère night, harking back to Paris and Manet, and there's another image taken in Studio 54 of a half-naked couple dancing in a clear bathtub, splashing in the water while they're in and amongst everybody else. These choreographed scenes start to resemble André Balazs' The Box at The Standard hotel in Los Angeles—in which people, who sometimes do not have clothes on, appear in the vitrine behind the desk of the concierge—or rather, The Box starts to resemble them.

And yes, I understand that the very fact of celebrities starring in the images explains why the photos stay *proper*. A celebrity's reputation can make or break their career and totally override their talent (and to be fair to them, any activity that showed them veering away from heterosexuality in clubs that were more welcoming to LGBT+ guests, for example, might have been bad for business). I'm just personally surprised that none of the edgier moments broke through. That would have made me like the photos more. Like, give me a bucking bronco instead of all these horses. That would have been chaotic. Nan Goldin's 1979 shot of *Cookie and Millie in the Girl's Bathroom at the Mudd Club* shows them side-by-side on toilets. I recognise it. I've done it. It's sweet to piss in proximity to each other. But when I trawl back through art history, I want to gasp and I never do.

In the UK, Denzil Forrester was creating drawings that lasted the length of a record. Setting himself up in dance halls in London in the early 80s, he would take sketches back to the studio to turn them into huge abstract paintings. The imagery is abstract but still locatable. He writes, 'in these clubs, city life is recreated in essence: sounds, lights, police sirens, bodies pushing and swaying in a smoke-filled room.' I give up. The abstraction actually feels more sincere in some ways: people turned into spirits made of light and colour embody, and transcend, the atmosphere Forrester describes. I like these but they are too... beautiful for me to really connect with them. They have an edge but one that is sanded down by time. Still, we're getting there. The scenes are getting recognisably modern and loosening up somewhat.

In the photo world, there are plenty of artworks set in house parties and raves, such as Anna Fox's series *Afterwards*, made between 1983 and 1996. In Fox's work, we can see bare-footed sleeping bodies tucked awkwardly around houses. Someone curled up in a foetal position on a carpet after the night is done. These images land in a category of their own. They are free and filthy and vulnerable, because people partying outside of official venues can take it so much further; it's cheaper, for one, and there's no one telling you what you can and can't do.

Chaotic House Parties is just waiting to be made. But we're not here for the houses, so back to the clubs we go.

Wolfgang Tillmans was there to document club culture in Germany after the fall of the Berlin Wall in 1989. Important work considering both the socio-political history and the no photo policies, many of which are still in place today. Picture make-up evaporating off of faces, latex, bumbags. Black leopard print dyed onto a shaved turquoise head. It's fashionable stuff, recording the kind of dance that's essentially exercise. In a Crack Magazine podcast, Tillmans said, 'For me, photographing queer spaces isn't voyeurism. I feel I have a duty to preserve it.' There is a closeness to the work but it's still protective, often carefully anonymised with the images taken from behind. I should say, I do prefer being on this end of the high-definition spectrum. Plus, I like that I can picture my own friends in these photos, the ones who look good from every angle.

Yeah, a lot of old nightlife art is boring, but I don't think these last few pieces are. I don't think Mark Leckey's *Fiorucci Made Me Hardcore* from 1999 is boring. I like watching it. It makes me feel excited. The film, which is available to watch on YouTube if you've still got your phone handy, collages tape footage of underground raves and Northern Soul parties from the 70s, 80s and 90s. Heady cuts and cropping mimic the unstable, drugged up atmospheres of clubbing at the time, and there are shots that show crushed bottles on the abandoned dance floors once the night is over. Pure exhaustion. It's a tight piece that praises the distinct spiritualism of the night, albeit with the kind of Fine Art handling that makes everything look cool and considered. Ridicule was not the aim at all.

Wu Tsang's widely exhibited 2012 film *Wildness* has the same fatal flaw. Respect! Reverence! The documentary portrait of the late Silver Platter nightclub in L.A. examines the dynamics of the Latinx/LGBT+ communities who once gathered there. It's four-dimensional, relational; and because of the documentary's subjectifying position, it comes closest to the realism I find myself wanting from artists who dabble in nightlife. But it's still an artwork isn't it, and maybe that conceptual framing is what's getting in the way of what I really want.

Because once we get past the millennium, we don't need to limit our nightlife search to the output of artists. By that point, the general public had already been granted compact digital cameras and camera phones. Paparazzi were out and about ruining lives. Google Images was now in existence, and social media was spreading like a bad rash. Even though artists still took club culture as a starting

24th February 2023:
@ClubPhotos_ posts a picture of a white woman posing for the camera at a club night called 'throb', lowercase 🕺 She doesn't have her hands on her hips 🪩 She isn't pouting 🍸 She isn't turning to the side to make her bum stick out 🎵 She is close to the camera, hands up to her face, the tips of both index fingers disappearing behind her eyeballs 💊 We can see the full circumference of her eyes which are now totally unimpeded by lids—eyes which appear seconds away from popping out of the sockets completely and dangling on this woman's cheeks 💃 It's body horror in the club tonight; throb, throb, throb 🎉

point for their inspiration, they weren't the only ones with the scoop anymore. Documentation was being produced at an exponential rate by everybody all of the time. Democracy! The whole world was unconsciously taking part in the creation of historical documents. And with the boom in conspicuous surveillance cameras installed everywhere, people were just a lot more accustomed to being photographed, especially in England. We had no choice in the matter. There's a camera in the offy, in the shops, in schools, hospitals, funeral parlours. You see yourself on a big screen when you walk into Tesco before you even see any of the food. We're in so many photos we don't consent to and in the backgrounds of others without even knowing (or caring).

And this is all I have known. That and the terrifying result of the social media rash we got infected with—the one that made us think of ourselves as special individuals with the potential to be paid for simply being who we are (as long as we share everything about ourselves on the internet, look normatively sexy, and market our personal brand to anyone who will listen). No one wants to be paid for doing what they don't want to do. But that's capitalism, baby! It's also the reason so many people drink; they want to temporarily lose their minds to free themselves from that ball and chain degradation, if only for an evening. So, when nightclubs began hiring in-house photographers, it made a lot of sense. Business sense, philosophical sense. Nightclubs created an attraction for customers who then had access to high quality photos of themselves that they could use on their internet profiles, including private dating profiles. These photos came with a high-flash high-colour allure that was reminiscent of a paparazzi shot. They made us feel like we were the celebrities worthy of being photographed; like we were datable, beautiful, valuable, DSLR-able; good enough at being a person that maybe we could make a living just being ourselves. Have a YouTube channel. A Kardashian empire. A merch line. Wow.

Do you want a photo of yourself? Do you want to increase your own cultural capital? We were drunk and trying to hear the photographer over the music, so these questions sounded one and the same.

When punters paid for these, erm, glamorous portraits, they also participated in free marketing for the club. They might walk away with a print, a keyring or some other tat. But money wouldn't even come into it most of the time. The photographer would whack the logo of the club in the corner of the frame and upload the night's haul to an album on the venue's Facebook page. With so many photos being produced night on night, and then spread through tags and comments and dating profiles, clubs were easily increasing their reach. Anybody who saw a portrait would know where to go if they wanted the same treatment. Clubs became massive free-for-all photo booths—nightlife was no longer just about dressing up, drinking and dancing, but about capturing all of that on camera before it went to waste.

As these developments were shaping the experiences of club-goers, the internet was busy figuring out its own sense of culture—its structure, customs, and its own language, too. Memes became one way of playing around with sincerity, irony, imagery, and language in order to express yourself in social settings online where tone can't always be heard. As is their nature, they often start as one thing and become something completely different. One of the most popular meme formats that emerged over the early 2000s was based on the tabletop game *Dungeons and Dragons*. Part of the set-up of the game involves players creating their own characters with the help of alignment charts. These consist of two axes: one that plots lawful, neutral and chaotic personality traits against good, neutral and evil ones. Internet users appropriated this chart, swapped personality traits in and out, and began plotting characters, bands, TV shows, politicians, and even IRL friends against these metrics for their own amusement.

Eventually, as is the way with these things, the internet kept just one part of the meme: the word chaotic. The adjective began appearing frequently in meme-heavy internet circles, circles where gimmick accounts are familiar on the timeline. Gimmick accounts are parodies on social media of real people or fictional characters, as well as subject-specific accounts and creative bots. I follow many of them because most tweets make me want to deactivate but gimmicks are always a treat, breaking up the feed with nonsense or art. I like @ukgranddesigns as an example. No context accounts share subtitled screenshots from TV shows, films and games that followers then save or quote tweet for their own meme-ends. There were plenty of other great accounts in this space—@arthurmorganbot for *Red Dead Redemption* quotes, @unicode_garden for beautiful character fields. Unfortunately Elon Musk took over Twitter and all of a sudden, large-scale API usage was forbidden. Thank God @ClubPhotos_ was being manually shared because...

It is out of these conditions that Chaotic Nightclub Photos was born. 🍷

The alignment chart evolution and the growing popularity of gimmick accounts led to a sudden 2020-2022 wave of pages with names like

@ChaoticFacebook, @chaoticcatpics, @chaoticdjs, @chaoticclubvids, and of course, Chaotic Nightclub Photos @ClubPhotos_. Each of these examples immediately attracted huge follower counts of the very-online users primed to enjoy them. Followers just like me.

We let loose because we need to. We are always taking photos of each other, and we are always having photos taken of us. We don't need to know each other in order to relate. We go online to talk in riddles and in-jokes. We want to be celebrities but really, we are just very embarrassing people. The popularity of Chaotic Nightclub Photos can tell us a lot. Art history? Yeah, there is plenty of information to be gleaned there, but the *mood* on the canvas was tame for so long. No Victorian children were at risk of exposure from drunken art, and I think that's a problem because I think it's a lie! Art should reflect the fullness of what humans get up to and that includes the humans in Ministry of Sound, Baa Bar, Revolution, Fabric, and that one square foot hole in Liverpool called Ça Va that sells 30 different flavours of tequila; a bar where I once thought I was going to die.

Fine Artists (by which I mean people who studied oil painting under masters, and us lot who stuck it out for a 3-4 year degree) have handled the aesthetics of nightclubs in their work with a consistent respectability that doesn't, and shouldn't, suit the subject matter. Artists love realism, but where are the masterpieces of people slipping on their own vomit? I want somebody to canonise a girl covertly pissing into a cup slap bang in the middle of a club, leaving it on a table full of other drinks, and then having it lashed at her when she walks back to her friends thinking she got away with it. Lydia Blakeley's series of paintings from her MFA in 2019 come close, depicting both sides of the action at The Grand National at Aintree Racecourse. We see horses crashing but we see men and women crashing too, drunk on the floor and leaning on each other for life support. Lydia, if you are reading this, please do nightclubs next. It's all right there on Twitter waiting to be painted.

I say that but I do think I have something against art. Maybe you could sense it when I did the art history section. Can't hide it. I'm an art critic or whatever, but sorting out these words over here is a lot more fun. I like art, don't get me wrong. But God, I find myself having all of these reactions, and getting excited to share those reactions, when the 'art' I encounter exists happily outside of an identified Fine Art establishment; when I don't need to rely on curators showing me what it is they think is important; when it's not even art, it's just content; or not even content, but just a thing that somebody made or did or found. The 'art' people make when they're not *meaning* to make anything *purposefully* meaningful can turn out much more interesting than the work artists try so hard to produce. There's something intensely sincere and perfect when a photo is just a photo. You know, camera roll, holiday snap. Photography equivalent of a butt-dial. When the value of the image is accidental, as a critic, it feels like finding a tenner on the floor. The raw stuff is more evocative than a stressed out artist contriving their own realism because it already happens to be real.

This is part of the reason I have an obsession with Chaotic Nightclub Photos. Somebody is taking the time to curate the very best of all the art that isn't explicitly art. There's a curatorial moment we're not privy to where disqualified club content is left on the cutting room floor. Maybe it wasn't chaotic enough. Maybe it was too chaotic. I dunno! I want to be there! Hear the thought process, feel the instinct. We're being shown somebody's interpretation of the word as they elevate certain videos and images, delivering their selection to one million people with no niceties, no press release, no trigger warning, nothing. Ta-da! It is a project that isn't a project because it's just a Twitter account and still, I *want* to call it a 'project' so badly. I want to discuss this treatment of photos in terms of curation because I have come from the Fine Art-dickhead-to-critic pipeline so I believe if I use this particular class of language, readers will take the account (and me) more seriously; as they will when the messaging comes published in a pamphlet through Rough Trade Books; as they will when they pass constant semi-colons that I'm not going to let anybody edit out, no way. It's just like, we know critics are going to write about exhibitions and films. That stuff's covered. But one million people are following this account, and what does that indicate? I'm going to use the remainder of this text to consider the public and personal value of Chaotic Nightclub Photos, and some of the problems with this *project*. 🥂

The popularity of anything is revealing. It's a data point that shows what we are needing from culture, prompting us to wonder why. For an account made in March 2022, the context is still mostly fresh in our collective memory. Lockdowns had been lifted, sort of. Nightclubs were back open but it was mandatory for people in the UK to present an NHS Covid Pass until 27th January 2022, and some venues were still asking for proof of them on a voluntary basis after that date had passed. What venues were even left? The Nighttime Industries Association and CGA Vanilla both report significant closures, less spending overall, and rising inflation putting pressure on the entire nighttime economy. Everyone was fucking skint.

A girl with thick fake eyelashes has an iPhone 12 disappearing into her mouth 💃 She is pouring a drink onto the back of it like Apple has re-invented the funnel 🪩 Two friends pose for the camera while a woman behind them sincerely tries to drink her water bottle from the bottom 🍸 A man dances with a lobster on his shoulder 🎵 Another man has backed up to a urinal to take a shit 🍺 A crowd has their hands up in the air and someone in the background is holding a literal radiator overhead 🎉 A man is performing at the club; one of the onlookers is a goat 🕺

The cost of living crisis in the UK began in late 2021 and it just... hasn't ended. Spending money on a night out has become more of a luxury given the fact a tin of beans now costs an arm and a leg; not to mention the price to keep your house warm so you don't just straight up die. For what it's worth, Russia also invaded Ukraine in February 2022 so life around that time was just dire.

That context only ups the chaos of Chaotic Nightclub Photos in my opinion. Makes sense that we'd want to see evidence of people having fun in busy venues to offset our own reality. Makes sense we'd want the reminder that having fun is a thing you can do. Or could do. Look at them, these crazy strangers up close and personal with one another. Touching! Kissing! Exchanging fluids in public! I think for some followers, observing the consensual, euphoric dirtiness of the nightclub might have worked to make them feel even more safe and clean at home. For others, the same chaos was filling a void, providing a surrogate vision of the scenes people haven't had access to for a while—scenes they still might not be able to jump back into given their bank account, their health, their new depression.

Chaotic Nightclub Photos holds a mirror up to our emotional state, but that's obvious. What's less obvious (because it's coming from my brain, I'm deciding it) is how comically representative the account is of this country's labour market. When somebody a hundred years from now does what I have done in tracking a history of artistic responses to nightlife, the 2010s era of DSLR-heavy nightclub photography is going to speak to economics more directly than any stage of the genre so far. These photos are the bleak outcome of a decentralised and informal gig economy of freelance photographers across the world who take on casual, non-contracted night jobs for supplemental income. The purpose is to produce marketing materials for the businesses that employ them. It's got nothing to do with making art and it's got nothing to do with the artist behind the camera. Slap a watermark on top, upload it, cue alienation from the product (especially when that product goes viral without you). It is a completely different approach to Manet labouring over portraits of barmaids in Paris in the 1800s. It's typical of the neoliberalism that art and plenty of other industries suffer under, because what's happening is no longer a labour of love. It's art to hire.

If we are to see this account as an exhibition of sorts, the account holder as the curator, the posts as the artworks on the walls, and the photographers as the artists (both the club pros and the camera-phone holders), Chaotic Nightclub Photos becomes a microcosm for the weird state the arts are in right now. Everyone is an artist but also nobody is, because there is no credit to be found anywhere. It's not about the person who made the thing, only about the joke in the post and its potential to become a meme in and of itself; for it to mean other things to other people in other places, and to go on to live a life far beyond its creator's reach. But by 'creator', do you think I mean whoever originally captured the content, or who the audience seems to pay more respect to—the person who gave it a funny caption, or who featured it on their specialised gimmick account, and therefore showed others the way into its value as a meme. It's like the respect given to the person who puts a playlist together rather than the musicians who recorded the songs; curators who are more famous than the artists they rely on.

It's easy to see Chaotic Nightclub Photos as an extractive, exploitative project. Curation is just a process of mining other people for the treasure they created. While all curation is extractive, it isn't always exploitative. That's where payment comes in. If we look to the YouTube equivalent of something like this—the compilation channel—YouTubers such as Daily Dose of Internet do in fact buy the rights to the clips that they share. I reckon that's partly because the presence of AdSense means viewers are versed in the business of the platform, and they know money is being made off the back of them. Twitter does not have anything like that in place so content is shared like it's the wild west. If no one is making money, it's less bad I suppose. But it's certainly still not equal.

The effect of dropping art into the social media slipstream is to accept letting go of it completely, because you cannot control what other users are going to do with your content. Artists are having to reckon with thoughts like, 'is it more worthwhile to have an artwork go viral without you than have it go nowhere at all?' All the while, they are losing more and more control, and audiences seem to be caring less. Artists are losing control of their rights, identity, autonomy, authenticity—a process that is fast-tracked by machine learning and the absolute plasticine shite that artificial intelligence systems are throwing up. It's just a matter of time before gimmick accounts like Chaotic Nightclub Photos produce their own generated content instead of waiting for real people in real clubs to play up to real cameras.

I am torn, I am torn. It's good and it's bad, like everything really. Emblematic of the bad practices that make being an artist basically impossible, yes. On the other hand, I kinda love what it's doing for audiences. The formula for seeing art usually involves a person going to a museum where they stand in front of an art object, look at it and assess whether they feel anything before moving on with their day. The art is there because the institution bought it, stole it, rented it, or commissioned it to be made. The artist is usually somebody who enjoys a stack of privilege, and the art they're sharing is an inoffensive bit of research or expression that everyone is used to seeing in a museum setting. No surprises here. You just might have to buy a ticket to see it.

The museum probably got funding because this particular exhibition fulfils some higher-level cultural strategy that the museum needs to pretend to care about so that everyone can be paid. Yeah, money needs to be made, and popular names sell tickets; family exhibitions also do well. When it comes to institutional art experiences, we're not being given a tailored cultural experience based on what we need in our gut(s). We're seeing what the museums need to show us in order for the place to stay in business. Same thing happens with television programming, cinema, record deals, book deals. No risk, no naughtiness, just Marvel, Picasso and Netflix.

To that end, I think it's liberating for people to witness the vulgarity of something like Chaotic Nightclub Photos. Vulgarity is getting harder to come by! Even online, censorship and moderation systems are ready to delete anything remotely spicy. But vulgarity has its place. People are weirdos and they should be seen as such. God, it's even liberating to me that the posts are anonymously curated. I obviously tried messaging to see if whoever it is, or whoever they are, wanted to talk for this pamphlet and I got nothing. Good. Means there's no one to blame. Might also be freeing to *not* have credit attached to each image, not just for the culture but the photographers too, who might not want to be associated with the imagery. Maybe it *was* only a job for them and they want to leave it at that, debris left outside of their main art practice (if they have one). Fine with me!

The other part of the freedom I feel has a lot to do with the online setting. Like, isn't it nice that I am talking about a cultural thing with printed reverence and you only have to go on your phone to share in that experience? You don't have to get a bus to a gallery, or a train to a bigger city, and then pay for a ticket, and queue up, and try to look at the thing over someone else's shoulder, and then think about how you're getting home and—yeah. I'm sorry to people who love a gallery day out but I have chronic fatigue and I don't live in a capital city, so I deeply appreciate it when interesting things are happening online; when it comes to me and I don't have to go to it. I wonder why big important museum directors don't invest more in the infinite, international audience they could have online. Gallery visitor numbers are still struggling to return to pre-pandemic heights... now feels like the right time to look at Twitter accounts with one million followers to see what it is people are responding to.

(I want to say this last thought in brackets, and if the font could be smaller I'd like that very much, because it could be another essay but: it's sort of liberating that no money is exchanged between the parties involved. I'm not supposed to say things like that, I'm supposed to be on the side of The People. But do you know what I hate more than curatorial exploitation? The fact that money even exists. I just think that the single purpose of Chaotic Nightclub Photos, its speed, and its blatancy put into perspective how brutally institutionalised culture has become. It's more organic to approach it in this freehand way; as though scrolling the account is the same as going through someone's coin collection (but then coins wouldn't exist if we got rid of money. But you get the point). Just, images and videos of drunk people in the chaotic category have an anarchic quality to them. Fuck the rules of the nightclub, fuck the rules of our mortal bodies. I wish the world this imagery was being made in could welcome that anarchy, or meet it in terms of display. Can't have it coming to us via Twitter. Not via Elon Musk. *Spit on the ground. Big spit!*).

Okay, are you ready for the stickier side of this essay? You might have been waiting for me to bring this up. Chaotic Nightclub Photos calls into question the ethics of consent. I'm sorry but it does. I opened this piece by describing a woman being felt up from behind by a man in the middle of a crowded dance floor. Between the couple in a state of rapture, the potentially high best friend off to one side, and the rogue old man entering from stage right, it's a once in a lifetime shot. At the beginning of this text, I said the girl had her eyes closed in pleasure. I just described the scene a second time and claimed the pair were in a state of rapture, but I am making huge assumptions. I don't know if she was frozen, eyes closed for reasons other than happiness—fear, shame, dissociation. For all I know, they all have it framed. Who knows how they feel about having such an intimate moment bouncing around the internet or written down like this. But I'll tell you what, I can remember how I felt when something similar happened to me.

When I was in sixth form, I was seeing a boy from another school who had a bit of a reputation. He'd slept with loads of girls, cheated on most of them, leaving a heap of scorned teenagers in his wake. I had dated few and far between, hadn't been drunk very much, and I did not yet know my limit. I just did my homework like a good little nerd. Read books, played games, and went to sleep in my own bed every night. Wasting my youth! Until one Friday night after school, The Boy took me to an 18th birthday party in a bar next to Lime Street Station where I didn't know anyone and nobody knew me.

I woke up not knowing what had happened that night but whatever, I was sure I'd had a good time and I didn't think much of it. I was young enough to think it was normal that I didn't remember anything when I was drunk. Brain just stopped recording. God bless me. Anyway, I was sat in the common room the following Monday and I saw a photo on Facebook (that dates it, wow). The photo showed a girl straddling The Boy Everyone Had An Opinion About upstairs at the party everyone from the other school had been to at the weekend. The comments were mounting. *Who was she?* It was happening on Twitter, too. Subtweets from people I didn't know. Speculation and judgement. Everybody was gossiping and my heart was beating fast, because the girl had long brown hair, a tight blue dress on, huge white Jeffrey Campbell Litas, and unfortunately, it was me—getting hot and heavy at the 18th birthday party.

I'm sure I was having the time of my life. I was bladdered, young and horny. It's not like I could be those things in my own house, or in his. We made do! I wouldn't have been thinking about anyone else in the bar, which would have been easy because I didn't know them. I was too drunk to be thinking about that stuff. I was too busy being 17. Empowered. Free. I was absolutely fine with my conduct *in the moment*. I look more than fine in the picture. But when I saw myself in the light of a Monday school day—when I saw the witch-hunt that had started, I was mortified. I was a bit scared too. I didn't want to be online like that, and if they found my name and said my name, then I would forever be attached to the picture. And fuck that.

I felt shame I didn't want to feel. Shame I didn't even really believe in! Suddenly, I didn't want The Boy's exes to see the picture because then they might think things about me that I didn't agree with. And then I was annoyed with myself for getting with This Boy I'd Eventually Regret because I already knew he'd pissed these girls off. The whole thing was only having a local internet moment because of him, and them, and the fact they desperately needed to know who he was currently seeing so one of them could later swill me in a club for being the scouse "Jolene."

Anyhow, I found myself caught in a web. Panicking but didn't want to tell my friends about it because I was embarrassed. I wanted the picture to be taken offline but I didn't know how to request that without outing myself. I resented whichever knobhead had taken the picture, knowing full well that if I had seen people getting frisky at a party, I probably would have taken a picture of them without thinking of the consequences. In the end, the boy saw the picture and

A boy with the fresh cheek of a horny first year student holds his phone above his head and points at it 🎉 On the screen, he has taken a photo of himself and written the word 'shag?' A second photo taken from behind his back shows a girl replying with a message on her own phone 🎵 It says 'NO' in bold yellow letters 💃 The reject has changed his pointing hand to a middle finger 🕺 There is a watermark in the bottom centre of both images that says 'feVer & Boutique, Plymouth, Photos by Ashleigh Pay 🍸' Thank you, Ashleigh 🍺

did the rounds telling everyone to delete it. We made it official soon after so the exes knew who to internet-stalk, and that was that.

I share this very random 2012 piece of gossip in an attempt to humanise the Chaotic Nightclub Photos girl beyond the meme she has become. Photo-taking can be such a buzzkill. Nobody asked me if it was okay to post it, and similarly, clubbers don't get to see the pro's memory card before they upload their night's work. If people did get to sign off on photos, I doubt the chaos accounts would exist. Because yeah, it's funny when it's an obvious friend-upload, but it is much funnier when the image has been processed by a professional; when it subverts the straight-laced marketing strategy and becomes an anti-capitalist, anti-drinking, anti-UK, anti-advertising intervention. But if people did get to sign off on photos, maybe the Renaissance-adjacent imagery wouldn't exist either. Does the threat of losing the chaotic but beautiful imagery make you care less about consent? I think that I appreciate Chaotic Nightclub Photos because I *don't* know the stories behind each of the posts. But if I stop for even a minute to consider how I would feel if some embarrassing or traumatic picture of me was being shared on that scale, at my expense, replicated into memes and so on... the potential for public and private shaming, domestic violence, potential employment or dating issues... yeah, criticism can be a buzzkill too. Because not only does this club content end up on meme pages like Chaotic Nightclub Photos (where I have seen entire genitals for the record), but explicit, sexual clips are put on Pornhub and Reddit. Imagine if that straddling photo of me had been a video instead? I would have cried.

When I was reading about the Wolfgang Tillmans series I referenced in the art history section, I ended up learning more about the no photos policies that are standard across clubs in Berlin. It made me pause because there are always replies under Chaotic Nightclub Photos tweets from people laughing to themselves because they can instantly tell a lot of the content is coming out of the UK. The internet can change how someone acts in public. I know it has become a deterrent for me. But it doesn't have to be this way. I found a quote that's worth sharing from Lutz Leichsenring of the Berlin Club Commission in which he says, 'Clubs that protect guests' privacy by means of a strict photography prohibition ensure that the participants of the events show more openness and act without a façade.' Doesn't that sound better? The events in the UK that approach photo policies with the same respect are usually sex and kink-related.

I should also note that Chaotic Nightclub content seems to only be coming out of clubs that do not cater to any particular demographic. Professional club photographers are not as common in gay bars where management knows that their customers could very well not be out; where photographing people without their consent could have immediately dangerous consequences; and where the community coming to them need the club as a space where they can 'show openness and act without a façade' because public and professional life involves an alienating, exhausting, and deeply unfair amount of code-switching. There is also the fact that platforms like Instagram are more likely to censor queer imagery, so it might be a waste of money anyway. Imagine if 'straight bars' followed this lead… I think people would be happier for it, even though that would mean the end of the reason I'm even writing this. But the internet is a big place and there's plenty of other content to enjoy.

Wait, have I written myself out of even liking this account? I don't know if I ever liked it in a clean cut way. It was something I needed to deal with, like there was an uncomfortable knot that I had to take time untangling before I knew what was what. And there is still some enjoyment remaining. It is a relief to remember that culture can form outside of established spaces. It was, and is, a salve to the pandemic, falling under the same category for me as shit rainbows scribbled by children in windows and even shitter cakes baked in the shape of politicians' faces. I appreciate that it sent me back through time, hoping to find Chaotic Nightclub Art that might reassure me that we've always been like this, although my results are inconclusive because I'm not built for history. I've never read a blue plaque in my life. I also appreciate the thought that Chaotic Nightclub Photos implies the existence of Lawful Nightclub Photos, Neutral Nightclub Photos, Good Nightclub Photos and Evil Nightclub Photos. It also implies the existence of Lawful Good Nightclub Photos, Neutral Good, Chaotic Good, Chaotic Evil; and so on.

The account reminds me of how much I used to enjoy Tabloid Art History, a gimmick account that closed down a few years ago. It would share pictures side by side: Britney Spears at a Del Taco drive-thru in 2007 next to *David with the Head of Goliath* by Caravaggio, c.1607. Made people laugh, made people learn; made me feel connected through space and time with the immaterial people inside paintings. I found myself doing this when I wrote the introduction comparing the girl to a Pre-Raphaelite but matching up contemporary images with allegorical scenes from way back when, is fun and emotional too. I would follow an account called

Nightclub Art History so fast. If anyone still has their phone to hand, they should see if the @ is available, quick. When I look through Chaotic Nightclub Photos, I sometimes feel the Renaissance-detector buzz in my head and I get excited, because these accidental compositions elevate our nonsense into important artefacts—like we're seeing something from a story; something to be painted, framed, and kept forever.

I can celebrate liberation, and I can be grateful for how much the account has inspired in me personally—11,000 words of inspo—but I cannot know the cost at which this is coming to me because the freedom is very much dependent on the mystery of it all. The account, each post, each person. And the thing is, I don't *want* to know the specifics. If I knew more, I wouldn't be able to enjoy my own conjecture. If I knew more, the people inside the photos would become too real. It would be more Lawful, wouldn't it? It just wouldn't be Chaotic at all.

The dance floor is empty apart from us and a handful of stragglers dotted around the room. I don't know how we've still got the energy. The staff behind the bar are pissed we're still here but we're too young to understand why. They turn the music off and a moment later the lights come up. Okay, then. Like the opposite of a parent turning lights off before bed. We lean against one another and close our eyes as we chug the last of our drinks. When we get to the top of the stairs, it is light.

We can hear birds, delivery vans. *What time is it?*

My phone has well ran out but yours is still on somehow, just about.

6A.M.

Haha. Oh. You call a taxi and we sit on a low wall together while we wait for it to arrive, feeling absurd in the daylight. We should be tired considering the fact we have not sat down for the past 7 hours, but we're still going—I stand up because my dress is so thin I can feel every sandpaper-edge of the brick.

We should get some pizza on the way home.

Nowhere is going to be open.

Oh, yeah.

Taxis arrive but they're not for us. The bar staff storm past. They got a head start before we realised the night was ending, or the day starting. Carry on waiting. We keep laughing about the past few hours. We lived a whole life. We saw a man in a suit do a slut drop and rip the crotch of his pants completely open. We saw everything. *Everything.* And then we didn't see anything because we had tears in our eyes.

Slut drop? I dunno what else you are supposed to say for that one.

Does it even matter if it's just the two of us here?

Someone else was doing card tricks in the middle of the dance floor, and I swear he was actually a magician because those cards were *flying*—or I was very, very drunk. You were drunk as well, though. I passed you a ciggie but you thought it was juicy fruit and you chewed it by accident. That girl next to us was filming when it happened. We should have got her name so we could have watched it back. That's so annoying.

We wait long enough that by the time the taxi arrives, we are sobering up. We feel self-conscious in the presence of a real adult operating heavy machinery. Think of tomorrow. Wonder what the photos are going to look like from tonight. I hope there are good ones. I've had the same profile picture for three weeks. I can't take it any longer.

I ask you to check the club's Facebook to see if tonight's album has gone up yet but as you go to unlock your phone, it dies. I don't want to admit how stressed that has made me—not knowing, wanting something I can't have, having to wait, needing to look good online because I need the love and I don't feel I've got it yet—but you're my best friend, and you can already see it on my face.

The photographer will be asleep anyway.

True, true. True.

The taxi pulls up to my house and the driver asks for a tenner. He says it's his last job of the night. I can't find my keys anywhere and I can't wake Mum up, she'll kill me. We sit on the front step, lean against one another and close our eyes.

Let's just check the photos tomorrow.

I think to myself, I wish we could take a photo right now.